Student Guide

for

Sexualities & Relationships

Third Edition

Ivy Chen, MPH

John P. Elia, Ph.D.

San Francisco State University

Kendall Hunt
publishing company

Contents

Section **1**

Attraction & Our Senses

Hormones' Complex Role in Human Sexuality

Discussion Questions

1. If there were a hormonal drug that could increase your love and faithfulness for another, would you take it? Why or why not?

2. Do you think that the results from hormone studies done on rodents can be accurately extrapolated to apply to humans?

Study Questions

1. According to the article, what would happen to men's behaviors if they got a nasal squirt of the hormone oxytocin?

2. How are the natural mating behaviors of the prairie voles different from the natural mating behaviors of the mountain voles?

True/False

T   F   1.   The bonding benefits of oxytocin and vasopressin can be used to help people with disorders like autism and schizophrenia to develop close relationships.

T   F   2.   According to the article, monogamy is very common throughout the animal kingdom.

Multiple Choice

1. According to neuropsychiatrist Louann Brizendine, which of the following is the "hormone of monogamy"?
   a. Oxytocin
   b. Vasopressin
   c. Dopamine
   d. Estrogen

Science Asks: What's the Attraction? Social, Biological Factors are in Play

Discussion Questions

1. What are the qualities you look for in a potential partner?

2. Do you feel that the results from studies that examine what heterosexual men and women find attractive can apply to gay men and lesbians?

Study Questions

1. What two things can help a man compensate if he is less physically attractive than the woman he is trying to court?

2. From an evolution standpoint, why would the "hourglass figure" (hips larger than the waist) be considered attractive in a female?

True/False

T   F   1.   According to the article, men focus more on the physical appearance of a potential mate, whereas women place more importance on personality.

T   F   2.   The research cited in the article confirms that opposites attract in terms of intelligence, family, and economic background.

T   F   3.   Online daters can easily tell if there is an attraction by just looking at photos in someone's profile.

Multiple Choice

1. What we consider to be attractive depends on
    a. biology.
    b. our parents.
    c. the mass media.
    d. all of the above.

2. Good earning power is considered attractive by
    a. women.
    b. men.
    c. both men and women.
    d. neither sex.

3. According to a study at the University of Rochester, what color worn by women was judged most attractive by men?
    a. blue
    b. red
    c. green
    d. yellow

Puckering Up Now Just Lip Service?

Discussion Questions

1. If a first kiss with a partner is not great, would you still continue the relationship, or would you end it?

2. What are the factors that would make a kiss good for you (how long it lasts, how much saliva exchange, sounds, how much tongue, etc.)?

Study Questions

1. According to Dr. Helen Fisher, what are the three distinctly different brain systems for mating and reproduction?

2. What five hormones and neurotransmitters are triggered to be released by kissing?

True/False

T F 1. Women are drawn to men whose immune system proteins are different than theirs, which is detectable from kissing.

T F 2. The majority of people kiss with their heads tilted to the left.

T F 3. When people kiss, their level of cortisol drops, which reduces stress.

Multiple Choice

1. What hormone is responsible for the sex drive in both men and women?
    a. Testosterone
    b. Estrogen
    c. Dopamine
    d. Norepinephrine

2. What other animals kiss besides humans?
    a. Pigs
    b. Dolphins
    c. Chimps
    d. Seals

Hold Me Tight

Discussion Questions

1. How important is touch to you as compared to your other senses?

2. When you have a fight with a partner, how do you go about making up with each other?

Study Questions

1. According to the author's experience, why do people have affairs?

2. Define what the author means by "demon dialogues."

True/False

T   F   1.   The author asserts that emotional isolation is traumatizing and dangerous for human beings.

T   F   2.   Men are often more sensitive than women to the first signs of a relationship connection breakdown.

T   F   3.   Touching your partner during an argument can instantly defuse anger and anxiety.

Multiple Choice

1. What part of the brain is considered our "fear center," triggered when we lose connection with a loved one?

    a. Amygdala
    b. Hypothalamus
    c. Pituitary gland
    d. Prefrontal cortex

2. When faced with conflict by a partner, men are inclined to

    a. actively fight.
    b. get defensive.
    c. withdraw themselves.
    d. remain calm and logical.

Section II

Relationship Decisions

Just Friends? Can a Platonic Relationship Turn Passionate? And if It Could, Would You Want It To?

Discussion Question

1. What has been your experience of turning a friendship into a romance?

Study Questions

1. According to the article, what is the primary reason why people do not attempt to change a platonic relationship into a romantic one?

2. Explain what the author means by "all friendships have ambiguous and changing boundaries."

True/False

T   F   1. We have different expectations for friends than for romantic partners, and flaws that are acceptable in a friendship may not be in a romantic relationship.

T   F   2. According to the article, timing plays a key role in determining whether the transition from friends to romantic partners is successful.

Multiple Choice

1. Author Kathy Werking states that when people look for a romantic partner, they want someone
    a.   with whom they are very familiar.
    b.   whom they do not know well and who has an air of mystery.
    c.   whom their parents will approve.
    d.   who is the complete opposite of themselves.

2. According to the article, what can be a powerful agent in turning platonic relationships into sexual ones?
    a.   A serious conversation confessing true feelings
    b.   Supporting a friend through a traumatic event in his/her life
    c.   Alcohol
    d.   Time apart from one another

College Relationships Veer from Tradition: Sex First, Dating Later

Discussion Question

1. Do you agree with the article that dating has "gotten all messy and uncertain" as compared to 50 years ago? Why or why not?

Study Questions

1. What is the "traditional, proper" order of courtship as compared to the sequence of romantic milestones today?

2. How did the invention of effective birth control such as the pill affect dating and relationships?

True/False

T   F   1. According to J.W. Wiley, an instructor of a romantic relationships course, various duties in a healthy relationship should naturally fall to one gender or the other, such as the expectation that the man should pay for dinner or initiate sex.

T   F   2. Due to evolution, men are more biased towards short-term relationships whereas women are more biased towards long-term relationships.

Multiple Choice

1. According to the article, which of the following qualities would a woman value the most in a partner?
    a. Physical strength
    b. Sense of humor
    c. Intelligence
    d. Dependability

2. A disadvantage cited regarding the use of the Internet to find romance is
    a. the danger of scammers and sexual predators on the Internet.
    b. people posting inaccurate representations of themselves on Internet-dating profiles.
    c. spending too much time on the Internet.
    d. the loss of face-to-face social skills as people rely more on online interactions.

New Research Says Women Bitterly Regret One-Night Stands

7

CHAPTER

Discussion Question

1.   What are your feelings about one-night stands?

Study Questions

1. According to Professor Campbell's research, why is a man not likely to settle down with a woman with whom he has had only casual sex?

2. What are some of the societal attitudes that have led to an increase in women having one-night stands?

True/False

T   F   1. Women regretted one-night stands only when their hopes for a more permanent relationship to follow the night of sex were not met.

T   F   2. According to the article, men have the same standards for long-term and short-term partners.

Multiple Choice

1. According to an online anonymous survey,
    a. the same number of men and women regretted one-night stands.
    b. more than twice the number of women regretted one-night stands as compared to men.
    c. women were 10 times more likely to regret one-night stands as compared to men.
    d. men regretted one-night stands more than women.

2. What would increase a woman's "mate value"?
    a. Shunning casual sex
    b. Simultaneously having two or three long-term partners
    c. Having sex on a first date
    d. Having sex with only handsome men

The Young and the Restless: Why Infidelity Is Rising Among 20-Somethings

CHAPTER 8

Discussion Question

1. What behaviors (sexual or otherwise) would you count as "cheating"?

2. According to the article, cheating peaks within six months of the birth of a first child. What do you think accounts for this surprising statistic?

Study Questions

1. What accounts for a greater level of "secrecy" when starting affairs in the modern era?

2. According to the article, why would having more monogamous relationships before marriage increase the chance of cheating within marriage?

3. According to the article, why would maintaining friendships with friends of both sexes after marriage increase the chance of cheating?

True/False

T   F   1.   According to the article, more women than men under the age of 30 cheated on their spouses.

T   F   2.   Despite the rise in infidelity, attitudes against adultery have gotten firmer, with more than 90 percent of people believing that cheating on a spouse is always wrong.

Multiple Choice

1. Marriage counselor Diane Sollee states that the increase in infidelity is due to
   a. people wanting more sex.
   b. marriage meaning less to people.
   c. more opportunity to develop intimacy with someone else.
   d. people getting married at younger ages than the last generation.

2. Research shows that cheating peaks right around
   a. six months of marriage.
   b. three years of marriage.
   c. seven years of marriage.
   d. ten years of marriage.

Lost Love—Guess Who's Back?

Discussion Question

1. Have you ever "Googled" an ex, and what were the results or consequences?

Study Questions

1. Why are romantic reunions more common and more easily accomplished than in the past?

2. Why do people often gravitate back to their first loves?

3. What are some of the uncontrollable circumstances that separated former partners in their youth, causing them to feel that their separation was unjust?

4. Define what the "autobiographical memory bump" is and how it affects our emotions about our first love relationships.

True/False

T F   1. When former partners reunite, their relationship tends to be more enduring and to have a much lower divorce rate than the general public.

T F   2. Threats to a relationship can actually increase feelings of longing, causing separated lovers to want to reunite desperately.

T F   3. Having had a past relationship with a partner, most people understand what to expect and are fully prepared for the impact that seeing an ex will have on their lives or current relationships.

Multiple Choice

1. According to Dr. Helen Fisher, when a lover is absent, our brain cells prolong their activities of secreting the chemical ______________, intensifying our passion to reunite.
    a. Dopamine
    b. Serotonin
    c. Oxytocin
    d. Prolactin

2. What percentage of lost-love reunions studied by the author involved extra-marital affairs?
    a. Approximately 20%
    b. Approximately 40%
    c. Approximately 60%
    d. Approximately 80%

Section 

Sexualities in the Adult Years: Being Single, Living Together, Marriage, Divorce

Lone Stars: Being Single

Discussion Question

1. Could you be satisfied being single your entire life? Why or why not?

Study Questions

1.   According to social historian Stephanie Coontz, why are women today less willing to get married as compared to men, or to women from a generation ago?

2.   Define the term "matrimania."

3.   What are some of the stereotypes associated with being single?

4.   What are some of the possible benefits of being single?

True/False

T   F   1.   According to the article, most people in the United States will spend more of their adult lives single than married.

T   F   2.   The banking industry today continues to discriminate against single women and makes it difficult for women to qualify for home loans.

T   F   3.   Psychologist McGrath finds that single men and women are often more sexually adventurous.

Multiple Choice

1.   Nowadays, many single people are no longer waiting for Ms. or Mr. Right to
   a. buy houses.
   b. have children.
   c. travel the world.
   d. all of the above.

2.   All of the following are important for a single person to feel fulfilled, EXCEPT
   a. satisfying work.
   b. a supportive network of family and friends.
   c. a lot of money in savings.
   d. a connection with the next generation.

New Data—and New Views—on Living Together

Discussion Question

1. How does living together with a romantic partner without marriage fit in with your personal, family, cultural, and religious values?

Study Questions

1. What is a "serial cohabitor"?

2. According to sociologist Paula England, what are Americans' attitudes towards marriage, especially as compared to a country like Sweden?

True/False

T F 1. New data shows that when someone cohabits only with a future spouse, divorce rates are the same or lower than if they had not lived together before marriage.

T F 2. The majority of Americans now live together before getting married.

T F 3. According to sociologist Pamela Smock, most people live together for many years without leading up to marriage in the United States.

T F 4. The article states that San Francisco has a higher rate of unmarried partners living together as compared to the national average.

Multiple Choice

1. One reason cited as to why more couples are living together and delaying the wedding is

    a. people postpone marriage to achieve higher education.
    b. fewer couples want children, cited as a main reason for getting married.
    c. marriage as an institution is less respected by younger generations.
    d. weddings are expensive.

2. The main reason why partners move in together, even without plans for marriage, is

    a. to be able to spend more time together.
    b. due to economics.
    c. the convenience of having all their belongings in one place.
    d. to monitor the other partner's behavior to prevent him/her from cheating.

The Perils of Playing House

12

CHAPTER

Discussion Question

1. Do you perceive Americans to be generally approving or disapproving of two people living together without marriage? Why?

Name: ______________________________

Study Questions

1. Explain the "inertia hypothesis" and how it can contribute to a couple divorcing later on.

2. What are some tips the article offers to make moving in together a smoother transition?

True/False

T   F   1. Nowadays, about 5 million opposite-sex couples and more than 600,000 same-sex couples cohabit, making living together a much more common and normal choice.

T   F   2. According to sociologist Paul Amato, people have much higher standards about whom they marry than whom they live with.

T   F   3. Sociologist Susan Brown found that a cohabiting couple has a higher chance of getting married if the woman really wants to do so.

T   F   4. Sociologist Paul Amato states that couples who cohabit before marriage may be or become less traditional, which can translate to their willingness to consider divorce, which is traditionally frowned upon.

T   F   5.   About 80 percent of all cohabiters eventually get married.

T   F   6.   The article recommends combining your finances together as soon as you two move in together.

Multiple Choice

1. Why do people who live together, but may not be the best life partners, end up marrying anyways?
   a. Family pressure
   b. Accidental pregnancies leading to children
   c. Guilt—feeling like you owe it to your partner
   d. All of the above

2. In general, how does cohabitation affect children?
   a. Emotionally and academically, children of cohabiters do equally well as those with two married parents.
   b. Emotionally and academically, children of cohabiters do not do as well as those with two married parents.
   c. Emotionally and academically, children of cohabiters do even better than those with two married parents.
   d. There is not enough data to show the effects of cohabitation on children.

3. One suggestion to protect against the potentially harmful effects of cohabitation is to
   a. get engaged before moving in together so that your expectations of commitment are clear.
   b. leave both of your previous living quarters and get a new place together to prevent feeling territorial.
   c. set up a joint bank account to demonstrate that you are financially invested in being together.
   d. get a pet together so that you two can practice parenting.

First the Marriage, Then the Courtship

Discussion Question

1. What are your feelings about arranged marriages, and would you ever be open
    to having a marriage arranged for you? (Compare your thoughts before vs. after
    reading the article.)

Study Questions

1. How are arranged marriages today in countries like the United States different than in the past?

2. According to the article, how has the Internet-dating experience poised people to be open to trying arranged marriages?

True/False

T   F   1.   According to the article, arranged marriage is an outdated and increasingly unpopular way for modern young people to find a spouse.

T   F   2.   The matchmaker for an arranged marriage is always a parent of either the bride or groom.

T   F   3.   According to author Reva Seth, women in arranged marriages are mostly happy because they have realistic expectations about their partners.

T   F   4.   The article states that the common Western notion of romantic love and a perfect soul mate causes much dissatisfaction.

Multiple Choice

1. One advantage that arranged marriage may have is that an objective third party can match the couple for

    a. similar levels of attractiveness.
    b. shared values.
    c. economic backgrounds.
    d. reproductive potential.

2. In the article, Dr. Epstein made which of the following statements?

    a. Our best life partners are most accurately determined by our parents.
    b. Most people fall in love at first sight.
    c. Extremely compatible matches can be made through Internet dating using an extensive questionnaire.
    d. Love in a marriage can be "made" if we work on accepting our partner bit by bit.

Preparing for Divorce Pays Off: Realistic Look at What Life Will Be Like After Separation Can Make Couples Rethink Decision

14

Discussion Questions

1. If you were to get married, would you ever consider divorcing? If so, for what specific reasons?

2. Do you think that being a divorced person today is easier in the United States than it was 50 years ago? If so, in what ways?

Study Questions

1.　What accounts for the loneliness that divorced people usually experience?

2.　In what ways can Internet porn inflict damage on relationships?

True/False

T　F　1.　According to the article, being divorced ends up being more difficult than people anticipate.

T　F　2.　The article states that most divorced people remarry within four years of their divorce.

T　F　3.　Divorce can negatively affect your finances for the rest of your life.

T　F　4.　During couple's therapy, simply agreeing to forget past relationship injuries is not enough; couples must reach their underlying emotions and truly forgive their partner in order to mend their relationship.

Multiple Choice

1. The first question divorce educator Deborah Moskovitch asks someone contemplating divorce is:
   a. "Do you have a pre-nup?"
   b. "Are you sure your relationship is over?"
   c. "How much alimony do you want?"
   d. "Do you want full custody of the children?"

2. What percentage of second marriages ends up in divorce?
   a. 20%
   b. 40%
   c. 60%
   d. 80%

3. The article states that it may be impossible to pull a couple back from the brink of divorce if one partner has
   a. declared that he/she does not want children.
   b. filed for bankruptcy.
   c. been diagnosed with a terminal illness.
   d. had an affair.

The Next Same-Sex Challenge: Divorce

Discussion Question

1. Do you agree that same-sex couples should have the rights to marry and divorce? Why or why not?

Study Question

1.   Why was it so difficult for the lesbian couple Ormiston and Chambers to get divorced?

True/False

T   F   1.   The federal government recognizes only marriages between one man and one woman.

T   F   2.   In gay divorces, money or assets ordered by a judge to be given to a spouse can be subjected to income taxes, whereas they are not in a heterosexual divorce.

Multiple Choice

1.   The Defense of Marriage Act was signed into law by President
    a.   Barack Obama
    b.   George W. Bush
    c.   Bill Clinton
    d.   Ronald Reagan

Section IV

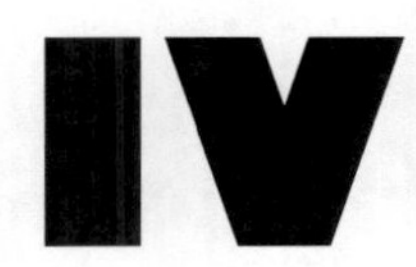

Challenging the Status Quo of Sexual Relationships

Queering Relationships: Toward a Paradigmatic Shift?

CHAPTER 16

Discussion Questions

1. How would you go about changing the institutional biases that exclusively celebrate and socially reproduce heteronormative relationships ?

2. List some examples and discuss how those in ostensibly heterosexual relationships can "queer" their relationships.

Study Questions

1. Why is it that some—perhaps even many—LGBT relationships are not considered "queer" relationships?

2. What are some advantages and disadvantages to queering relationships?

True/False

T   F   1.   The institutions mentioned in the chapter that have influenced relationship construction are medicine, religion, the law, politics, the family, and education.

T   F   2.   One way school-based sexuality education has helped to queer relationships is to focus on the abstinence-only approach.

T   F   3.   Same-sex marriage does not afford gays and lesbians even a little social approval, and certainly not even a few rewards.

T   F   4.   Queer relationships have been around forever.

Multiple Choice

1. Although marriages are ultimately formal legal contracts, they
    a. have to be tied to religious traditions of some sort.
    b. are oppressive socially and economically.
    c. are often shrouded in religious overtones and meanings.
    d. are not binding unless the City and County Recorder and Clerk of the Court agree.

2. According to the chapter *Queering Relationships: Toward a Paradigmatic Shift?*, perhaps the best example of material benefits resulting from being in a traditional relationship is
    a. tax benefits.
    b. being able to go on luxurious vacations.
    c. getting better jobs.
    d. having a great deal of social mobility.

3. Which following statement(s) is/are true based on the chapter *Queering Relationships: Toward a Paradigmatic Shift?*
    a. Authors of interpersonal communication textbooks are more negligent about mentioning and generally covering issues of gay and lesbian relationships than authors of general human sexuality texts.
    b. Overall, both the interpersonal communication texts and the general human sexuality texts fail to include the diversity of "real life" relationships.
    c. Homosexuality approaches legitimacy only in so far as it reflects middle-class conventional romantic norms.
    d. All of the above.

Redefining Our Relationships: Guidelines for Responsible, Open Relationships

Discussion Question

1. Why do you think most people prefer a monogamous relationship with one person to a polyamorous relationship with two or more people?

Study Questions

1. Define the "24-Hour" rule in the guidelines.

2. List four other rules presented in the guidelines.

True/False

T   F   1.   The patriarchal relationship paradigm puts your sexual partner, family, and friends all on the same level of importance.

T   F   2.   The author states that women, whether straight or queer, who seek sexual liberation are still labeled sluts or nymphos.

T   F   3.   The author maintains that open relationships are ultimately about sex.

T   F   4.   As a courtesy to a partner with whom you live, the author suggests leaving a note if you are not going to come home that night to be with another.

Multiple Choice

1. The author claims that her preference for open relationships is based primarily on
    a. her lack of commitment.
    b. her capacity to love many.
    c. her desire for lots of sex partners.
    d. her social statement of sexual liberation.

2. The author believes in all of the following, EXCEPT
    a. honest communication.
    b. respect for mutually agreed-upon rules.
    c. the concept of the soul mate.
    d. reinvention of commitment.

Section 

To Parent or Not To Parent?

Kids R Not Us— Embracing the Decision Not to Procreate

Discussion Questions

1. What do you think are the implications in using the term "childfree" instead of "childless"?

2. If your partner were to tell you that he/she does not want to have children, how would you react?

Study Questions

1. What social changes in the '70s challenged the notion that everyone must marry and have children?

2. According to the article, why do childfree people find it difficult to be open with other people about their decision to not have kids?

True/False

T   F   1. San Francisco has one of the lowest ratios of kids in any U.S. city.

T   F   2. According to the article, childfree people often spend more time caring for aging parents.

T   F   3. The process for a woman in her twenties to get sterilized by her doctor is relatively easy and quick.

Multiple Choice

1. According to Christine Fisher, who runs a childfree podcast, the public perception of people who are childless by choice is that they are
    a. free and independent.
    b. immature.
    c. cold and uncaring.
    d. ambitious and career-minded.

2. In a survey of childfree couples, all are top reasons why they chose not to have kids, EXCEPT
    a. independence.
    b. kids are a financial burden.
    c. greater marital satisfaction because they can focus more on their partner.
    d. they perceive the world to be a polluted and dangerous place.

Knocking Yourself Up

19

CHAPTER

Discussion Question

1. If Mr. or Ms. Right never showed up, would you consider becoming a single
    parent, either through adoption or reproductive technology? Why or why not?

Study Question

1. What accounts for the increase in single women having children through sperm donors?

True/False

T   F   1.   According to one of the largest sperm banks in the country, 60 percent of its clients are single females.

T   F   2.   Kids of single, older moms who got pregnant by choice, do much worse educationally and emotionally than kids who live with two parents.

Multiple Choice

1.   What is the statistic for U.S. babies born outside of marriage?
    a.   One in 25 babies is born out of wedlock.
    b.   One in 10 babies is born out of wedlock.
    c.   Two in 10 babies are born out of wedlock.
    d.   Four in 10 babies are born out of wedlock.

Section 

Finance & Romance

The Key to Wedded Bliss? Money Matters

Discussion Questions

1. What kind of lifestyle would you be satisfied with?

2. In a self assessment, how would you rate your savings and spending habits?

Study Questions

1. What does Betsey Stevenson, researcher of marriage economics, mean when she says that the "debates people have about money are code for how we want to live our lives"?

2. What are some steps to "run a home like a business"?

True/False

T   F   1. For centuries, marriage was for economic or political purposes rather than for love.

T   F   2. According to divorce lawyer Susan Winters, money is not a major factor in why marriages break up.

Multiple Choice

1. Which of the following is a financial decision?
    a. Having children
    b. Where you live
    c. Traveling/vacations
    d. All of the above

2. All of the following are guidelines to having a successful financial relationship with your partner, EXCEPT
    a. being supportive of each other's careers.
    b. yielding the financial planning to the partner with a stronger aptitude for money.
    c. when stuck between two divergent decisions, using a mediator.
    d. maintaining some financial independence; having some spending money of your own.

An Airfare to Remember: As the Cost of Travel Soars, Couples in Long-Distance Relationships Are Feeling the Pinch

CHAPTER

Discussion Questions

1. How do you define "long distance" —how many miles apart?

2. If you were separated from a long-distance partner by 350 miles (approximately the distance between San Francisco and Los Angeles), how often would you expect to have face-to-face visits, and who should do more of the traveling?

Study Questions

1. What are some commodities that have increased in price that put additional barriers to long-distance couples' ability to see each other face-to-face?

2. What are some strategies that the couples featured in the article used to maintain their long-distance relationship?

True/False

T   F   1. Relationship expert Greg Guldner says that if long-distance couples do not visit each other at least once a month, they are doomed to break up.

T   F   2. Long-distance couples are recommended to have 60-minute phone calls every day in order to stay close.

Multiple Choice

1. According to Greg Guldner, long-distance relationship expert, the average long-distance couple is separated by _______ miles.

    a. 125
    b. 550
    c. 1200
    d. 2500

2. Ultimately, couples in long-distance relationships stay together as long as

    a. the time apart from each under is under six months.
    b. the cost of each face-to-face visit is under $500.
    c. the distance between them is less than 500 miles.
    d. the time the couple spends together outweighs the burden and costs of being apart.

Section VII

Terminating Relationships

The Eight Stages of Ending A Relationship

Discussion Questions

1. Does gender, age, ethnicity, and sexual orientation influence how one experiences the stages of an ending relationship? If so, how?

2. Do you think it is possible to be friends with an ex?

Study Questions

1. How is the "We Can Work It Out" stage different from the "What Went Wrong" stage?

2. How is "Bargaining" different from "Obsession"?

True/False

T   F   1.   Both partners will feel "Pleasant Surprise" sometime within the first two stages of an ending relationship.

T   F   2.   Only the partner being left will experience "Bargaining."

T   F   3.   The partner choosing to end the relationship may feel "Regret."

T   F   4.   A person will likely experience tremendous anger during the "No Going Back" stage.

T   F   5.   The stage "I'm Not the Same Person" comes before the stage "We Can Work It Out."

Multiple Choice

1. The first stage a person experiences during an ending relationship is
    a. Denial.
    b. Resentment.
    c. Anger.
    d. Unexpected Relief.

2. Which statement is true regarding the stages of an ending relationship?
    a. The "Anger" stage comes near the end of the grieving process.
    b. Both partners will go through each of the stages at the same time.
    c. Only the partner ending the relationship will experience anger.
    d. Both partners will pass through the "We Can Work It Out" stage.

3. The last stage of an ending relationship is
    a. Depression.
    b. Regret.
    c. Harmony.
    d. Peace.

Answer Key

Chapter 1

T/F

1. T
2. F

MULTIPLE CHOICE

1. a

Chapter 2

T/F

1. T
2. F
3. F

MULTIPLE CHOICE

1. d
2. c
3. b

Chapter 3

T/F

1. T
2. F
3. T

MULTIPLE CHOICE

1. a
2. c

Chapter 4

T/F

1. T
2. F
3. T

MULTIPLE CHOICE

1. a
2. c

Chapter 5

T/F

1. T
2. T

MULTIPLE CHOICE

1. b
2. c

Chapter 6

T/F

1. F
2. T

MULTIPLE CHOICE

1. d
2. c

Chapter 7

T/F

1. F
2. F

MULTIPLE CHOICE

1. b
2. a

Chapter 8

T/F

1. F
2. T

MULTIPLE CHOICE

1. c
2. c

Chapter 9

T/F

1. T
2. T
3. F

MULTIPLE CHOICE

1. a
2. c

Chapter 10

T/F

1. T
2. F
3. T

MULTIPLE CHOICE

1. d
2. c

Chapter 11

T/F

1. T
2. T
3. F
4. T

MULTIPLE CHOICE

1. d
2. b

Chapter 12

T/F

1. T
2. T
3. F
4. T
5. F
6. F

MULTIPLE CHOICE

1. d
2. b
3. a

Chapter 13

T/F

1. F
2. F
3. T
4. T

MULTIPLE CHOICE

1. b
2. d

Chapter 14

T/F

1. T
2. F
3. T
4. T

MULTIPLE CHOICE

1. b
2. c
3. d

Chapter 15

T/F

1. T
2. T

MULTIPLE CHOICE

1. c

Chapter 16

T/F

1. T
2. F
3. F
4. T

MULTIPLE CHOICE

1. c
2. a
3. d

Chapter 17

T/F

1. F
2. T
3. F
4. T

MULTIPLE CHOICE

1. b
2. c

Chapter 18

T/F

1. T
2. T
3. F

MULTIPLE CHOICE

1. c
2. d

Chapter 19

T/F

1. T
2. F

MULTIPLE CHOICE

1. d

Chapter 20

T/F

1. T
2. F

MULTIPLE CHOICE

1. d
2. b

Chapter 21

T/F

1. F
2. F

MULTIPLE CHOICE

1. a
2. d

Chapter 22

T/F

1. F
2. F
3. T
4. F
5. F

MULTIPLE CHOICE

1. a
2. d
3. c